SHORT WALKS
MADE EASY

BRECON BEACONS/
BANNAU BRYCHEINIOG

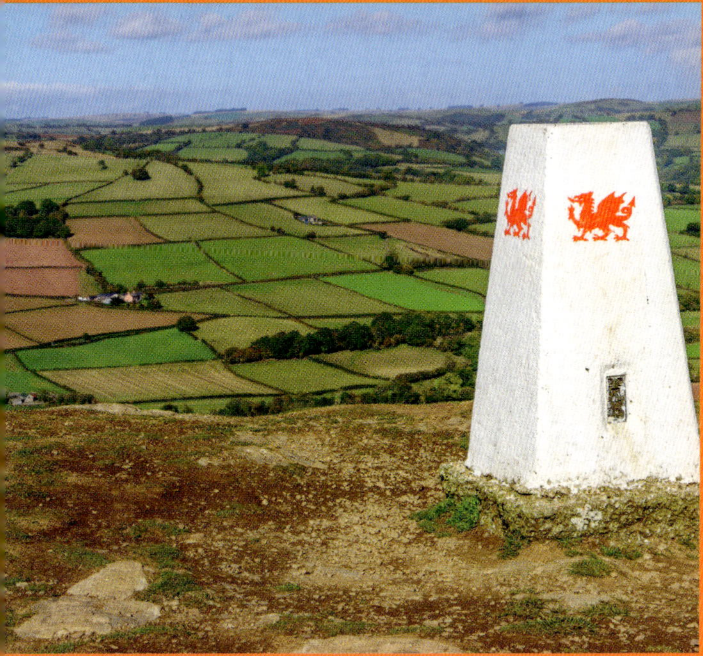

Contents

Getting outside in the Brecon Beacons		6
We smile more when we're outside		8
Respecting the countryside		10
Using this guide		11
Walk 1	Dinefwr Park	**14**
Walk 2	Waterfalls Walk	**20**
Photos	Scenes from the walks	26
Walk 3	Mynydd Illtud	**28**
Walk 4	Brecon Canal Basin and River Usk	**34**
Photos	Wildlife interest	40
Walk 5	Blaen-y-glyn	**42**
Walk 6	Brynich Lock to Talybont-on-Usk	**48**
Walk 7	Craig y Cilau	**54**
Photos	Cafés and pubs	60
Walk 8	Hay-on-Wye	**62**
Walk 9	Sugar Loaf	**68**
Walk 10	Castle Meadows	**74**
Credits		80

Map symbols	Front cover flap
Accessibility and what to take	Back cover flap
Walk locations	Inside front cover
Your next adventure?	Inside back cover

2 Short Walks Made Easy

Walk 1

DINEFWR PARK

Distance
2.1 miles / 3.4km

Time
1½ hours

Start/Finish
Dinefwr Park

Parking SA19 6RT
National Trust car park

Cafés/pubs
National Trust café

Medieval castle ruin, Jacobean mansion and scenic deer park

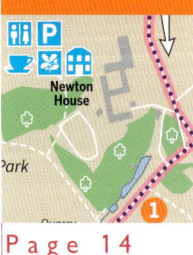

Page 14

Walk 2

WATERFALLS WALK

Distance
3.8 miles/6.1km

Time
3 hours

Start/Finish
Cwm Porth

Parking CF44 9JF
Cwm Porth car park

Cafés/pubs
Kiosk in car park

Thundering waterfalls; river and woodland birds; cave exploration

Page 20

Walk 3

MYNYDD ILLTUD

Distance
4.25 miles/6.8 km

Time
2¼ hours *CATCH A BUS*

Start/Finish
National Park Visitor Centre, near Libanus

Parking LD3 8ER
Visitor Centre car park

Cafés/pubs
Visitor Centre café

Pen y Fan and Corn Du mountain views; great visitor centre and café

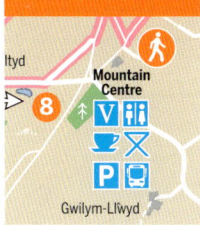

Page 28

Walk 4

BRECON CANAL BASIN AND RIVER USK

Distance
3.9 miles/6.3km

Time
2 hours *CATCH A BUS*

Start/Finish
Theatr Brycheiniog, Brecon

Parking LD3 7HL
Theatr Brycheiniog car park

Cafés/pubs
The Waterfront Café, Brecon

Gentle canal towpath and across-the-fields riverside walking

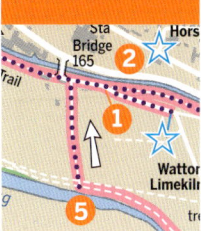

Page 34

Walk 5
BLAEN-Y-GLYN

Distance
1 mile/1.6km

Time
½ hour

Start/Finish
Blaen-y-glyn Isaf

Parking CF48 2UT
Blaen-y-glyn Isaf car park

Cafés/pubs
None (nearest café, Torpantau)

Plummeting falls and tumbling cascades in a wild and beautiful gorge

Page 42

Walk 6
BRYNICH LOCK TO TALYBONT-ON-USK

Distance
4.9 miles/7.9km

Time
2½ hours *CATCH A BUS*

Start Brynich Lock
Finish Talybont-on-Usk

Parking LD3 7YQ
The Hub, Penpentre, Talybont-on-Usk

Cafés/pubs
Pub at Pencelli; café and pubs in Talybont-on-Usk

Pretty, easy-going canal walk, with a lovely pub stop at half distance

Page 48

Walk 7
CRAIG Y CILAU

Distance
2.5 miles/4km

Time
1½ hours

Start/Finish
Llangattock Escarpment

Parking NP8 1LG
Car park off Hafod Road

Cafés/pubs
None (nearest in Crickhowell)

Towering cliffs, quarry remains and breathtaking Usk Valley views

Page 54

4 Short Walks Made Easy

Walk 8
HAY-ON-WYE

Distance
2.1 miles/3.4km

Time
1¼ hours

Start/Finish
Hay-on-Wye

Parking HR3 5BJ
Wyeford car park

Cafés/pubs
Hay-on-Wye

Relaxing riverside walk to a meadow, ideal for picnics or book reading

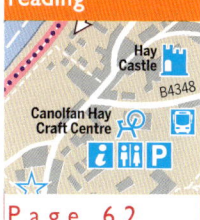

Page 62

Walk 9
SUGAR LOAF

Distance
3.8 miles/6.1km

Time
2½ hours

Start/Finish
Mynydd Pen y Fâl car park

Parking NP7 7LA
Mynydd Pen y Fâl car park

Cafés/pubs
None (nearest in Abergavenny)

A fabulous mountain walk best saved for the views on a fine day

Page 68

Walk 10
CASTLE MEADOWS

Distance
2.75 miles/4.4km

Time
1½ hours

Start/Finish
Abergavenny Railway Station

Parking NP7 5HF
Bus Station car park

Cafés/pubs
Abergavenny

Abergavenny's foodie delights; riverside meadow and castle ruin

Page 74

GETTING OUTSIDE IN
THE BRECON BEACONS

> " The beauty of the Brecon Beacons is that you don't have to climb mountains for wonderful mountain views

OS Champion
Phillipa Cherryson

Monmouthshire and Brecon Canal

A very warm welcome to the new Short Walks Made Easy guide to the Brecon Beacons — what a fantastic selection of leisurely walks we have for you!

Officially adopting its Welsh name of Bannau Brycheiniog in spring 2023, the Brecon Beacons National Park was established in 1957. It was the third national park in Wales and the tenth created in Britain. Covering 519 square miles across South Wales, the national park embraces the hilliest terrain in southern Britain, ranging from Llandeilo to Abergavenny, and from Hay-on-Wye to Merthyr Tydfil. Do visit the Mountain Centre (Walk 3) to discover more.

The beauty of the Brecon Beacons is that you don't have to climb mountains for wonderful mountain views. They are all around on the walks at Mynydd Illtud and Craig y Cilau. For energetic walkers, the ascent of Sugar Loaf rewards the uphill effort with stupendous views across the national park.

This is cascade country too, with some thundering torrents encountered in the Blaen-y-glyn gorge and on the Waterfalls Walk. The Usk Valley provides soothing riverside rambles from Brecon and Abergavenny, while you could spot wildlife from the towpath along the Monmouthshire and Brecon Canal. At Hay-on-Wye, why not combine a fine stroll around the Warren beside the river with some bookshop browsing?

History lovers can enjoy castles at Dinefwr Park and Abergavenny, and quarrying and industrial heritage at Craig y Cilau and Brynich Lock.

Phillipa Cherryson, OS Champion

WE SMILE MORE WHEN WE'RE OUTSIDE

Sugar Loaf

Whether it's a short walk during our lunch break or a full day's outdoor adventure, we know that a good dose of fresh air is just the tonic we all need.

At Ordnance Survey (OS), we're passionate about helping more people to get outside more often. It sits at the heart of everything we do, and through our products and services, we aim to help you lead an active outdoor lifestyle, so that you can live longer, stay younger and enjoy life more.

We firmly believe the outdoors is for everyone, and we want to help you find the very best Great Britain has to offer. We are blessed with an island that is beautiful and unique, with a rich and varied landscape. There are coastal paths to meander along, woodlands to explore, countryside to roam, and cities to uncover. Our trusted source of inspirational content is bursting with ideas for places to go, things to do and easy beginner's guides on how to get started.

It can be daunting when you're new to something, so we want to bring you the know-how from the people who live and breathe the outdoors. To help guide us, our team of awe-inspiring OS Champions share their favourite places to visit, hints and tips for outdoor adventures, as well as tried and tested accessible, family- and wheelchair-friendly routes. We hope that you will feel inspired to spend more time outside and reap the physical and mental health benefits that the outdoors has to offer. With our handy guides, paper and digital mapping, and exciting new apps, we can be with you every step of the way.

To find out more visit os.uk/getoutside

RESPECTING
THE COUNTRYSIDE

You can't beat getting outside in the British countryside, but it's vital that we leave no trace when we're enjoying the great outdoors.

Let's make sure that generations to come can enjoy the countryside just as we do.

 Leave no trace

 Keep dogs under control; bin and bag waste

 Do not light fires; only BBQ at official sites

 Leave gates as you find them

 Keep to footpaths and open access land

 Plan ahead for your trip

For more details please visit
www.gov.uk/countryside-code

USING THIS GUIDE

Easy-to-follow Brecon Beacons walks for all

Before setting off

Check the walk information panel to plan your outing

- Consider using **Public transport** where flagged. If driving, note the satnav postcode for the car park under **Parking**
- The suggested **Time** is based on a gentle pace
- Note the availability of **Cafés**, tearooms and pubs, and **Toilets**

Terrain and hilliness

- **Terrain** indicates the nature of the route surface
- Any rises and falls are noted under **Hilliness**

Walking with your dog?

- This panel states where **Dogs** *must* be on a lead and how many stiles there are – in case you need to lift your dog
- Keep dogs on leads where there are livestock and between April and August in forest and on grassland where there are ground-nesting birds

A perfectly pocket-sized walking guide

- Handily sized for ease of use on each walk
- When not being read, it fits nicely into a pocket...
- ...so between points, put this book in the pocket of your coat, trousers or day sack and enjoy your stroll in glorious countryside – we've made it pocket-sized for a reason!

Flexibility of route presentation to suit all readers

- **Not comfortable map reading?** Then use the simple-to-follow route profile and accompanying route description and pictures
- **Happy to map read?** New-look walk mapping makes it easier for you to focus on the route and the points of interest along the way
- **Read the insightful Did you know?, Local legend, Stories behind the walk** and **Nature notes** to help you make the most of your day out and to enjoy all that each walk has to offer

OS information about the walk

- Many of the features and symbols shown are taken from Ordnance Survey's celebrated **Explorer** mapping, designed to help people across Great Britain enjoy leisure time spent outside

- National Grid reference for the start point
- Explorer sheet map covering the route

OS information

SN 615223
Explorer 186

The easy-to-use walk map

- **Large-scale** mapping for ultra-clear route finding

- **Numbered points** at key turns along the route that tie in with the route instructions and respective points marked on the profile

- **Pictorial symbols** for intuitive map reading, see Map Symbols on the front cover flap

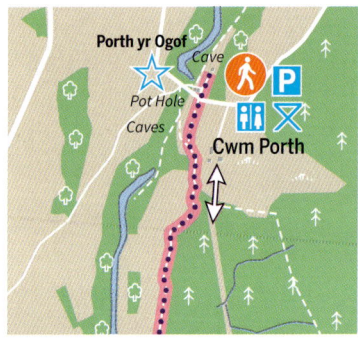

The simple-to-follow walk profile

- Progress easily along the route using the illustrative profile, it has **numbered points** for key turning points and **graduated distance** markers

- Easy-read **route directions** with turn-by-turn detail

- Reassuring **route photographs** for each numbered point

Walk towards the hut at the car park entrance and go past the barriers to the left of it.

Using QR codes

- Scan each QR code to see the route in Ordnance Survey's OS Maps App.
NB You may need to download a scanning app if you have an older phone

- OS Maps will open the route automatically if you have it installed. If not, the route will open in the web version of OS Maps

- Please click **Start Route** button to begin navigating or **Download Route** to store the route for offline use

Brecon Beacons

WALK 1

DINEFWR PARK

OS information

SN 615223
Explorer 186

Distance	2.1 miles/3.4km
Time	1½ hours
Start/Finish	Dinefwr Park
Parking	SA19 6RT National Trust car park
Public toilets	National Trust, at the start
Cafés/pubs	National Trust café and kiosk; picnic benches
Terrain	Mainly good, surfaced paths
Hilliness	Undulating, with a steeper climb/descent to/from the castle
Footwear	Year round

Located just a short distance outside the boundary of the national park, Dinefwr Park makes a magical place for a stroll. Centred on Newton House – an impressive 17th-century manor house – the park consists of 800 acres of hilly meadow and prime woodland, crowned with the ruins of an imposing 12th-century castle. There's an opportunity to walk among a herd of fallow deer in the deer park, and to enjoy a great café and restaurant.

Public transport

Bus and mainline railway services to Llandeilo, 1½ miles from 🚶: traveline.cymru (nearest bus stop on Carmarthen Road, at the end of Dinefwr Park drive, ¾ mile from 🚶)

Accessibility

Good accessibility, but the undulating route may favour powered chairs only. The boardwalk in the deer park, close to ❶, would suit manual chairs

Did you know? Newton House claims to be one of the most haunted homes in Britain and, over the years, there have been many reports of ghost sightings and other paranormal activity. Stories abound, including one of a ghostly butler named Walter and another of Lady Elinor Cavendish, a cousin of the lady of Newton House in the 1720s, who was strangled by a jilted lover.

Local legend Giraldus Cambrensis (aka Gerald of Wales, the 12th-century historian) tells of a local cleric who, when tasked to guide one of Henry II's men on a reconnaissance mission, actually took the potential invader by the longest route possible and subjected him to eating grass, convincing him it was the local way during hard times. It worked and the king's plan to attack Dinefwr Castle was abandoned.

Dogs

Welcome on leads in the outer park only. Dogs prohibited in formal gardens and deer park, so return from ❺ by your outward route. No stiles

Walk 1 Dinefwr Park

STORIES BEHIND THE WALK

Dinefwr Castle The imposing ruins of Dinefwr Castle stand on a craggy hilltop overlooking the beautiful Afon Tywi. The date of the fortress's original construction is unknown, but in the 12th century it was in the possession of The Lord Rhys, ruler of the ancient south Wales kingdom of Deheubarth. It fell under English control after his death and remained so, despite the efforts of Welsh leader Owain Glyndŵr in 1403. It is now a Grade I-listed building, managed by CADW (the Welsh historic environment service).

Dinefwr Park The 800-acre Dinefwr Park is both a Site of Special Scientific Interest (SSSI) and a National Nature Reserve (NNR). The unique woodland habitat is home to some of the oldest trees in Britain, with some thought to be over 700 years of age. It hosts a diverse range of habitats, including flower-rich hay meadows, dense woodland, bog woodland and wet meadows, as well as an impressive array of flora and fauna (see pp18–19).

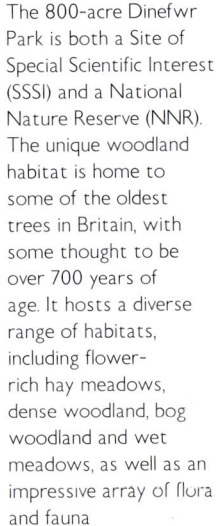

Newton House

➡ From the main car park, locate the small green National Trust hut and with this to your right, head downhill on a broad track to cross a cattle grid.

1 ➡ Keep **straight ahead** to a fork and bear **right**, passing through a succession of gates until a final gate gives access to open ground, with views of the castle ahead.

Short Walks Made Easy

⭐ **Llandeilo** The Carmarthenshire town of Llandeilo sits on the Afon Tywi, just outside the Bannau Brycheiniog/Brecon Beacons National Park. It's named after 6th-century Saint Teilo, a contemporary of Saint David, who established a small monastic settlement here. He was later buried in the town. It's a lovely, typical Mid Wales town and well worth exploring.

🏠 Newton House

At the heart of Dinefwr Park sits the magnificent Newton House – a Grade II-listed building constructed during the medieval period. The current building was completed in 1660, under the command of Edward Rice, the great grandson of Rhys ap Gruffudd, though it was further modified during the 18th century when the turrets and battlements were added. The gardens and deer park were landscaped by Capability Brown.

Dinefwr Castle

2 ▸ Keep **ahead** to climb to another gate and continue up through woodland to a T-junction.
▸ Turn **right** and continue uphill until you reach the castle, passing the remnants of the moat.

3 ▸ Explore at your leisure then return to the castle entrance and retrace your footsteps back down through the wood onto the open ground again. Continue towards the gate at the bottom of the hill.

1 mile

Walk 1 Dinefwr Park

NATURE NOTES

Spring in Dinefwr is a colourful time of year with bluebells carpeting the woodland floor, and celandines and wood anemones adding a touch of yellow and white to the scene.

The bog woods and lily pond can be enjoyed from a 500-yard-long boardwalk, which can be accessed when the deer park is open, and the trees and canopy are home to some fascinating bird species, including the diminutive treecreeper, as well as more common corvids, such jays and magpies.

The boardwalk also provides a good viewing point for the fallow deer that live in the park. These medium-sized deer are easily identified by their red-brown colour and white spots, though there is usually some variation in a herd. They actually originate from Asia but are now the most common deer in Wales. Keep your eyes open near ❷ for the impressive, Ent-like, roots of the beech trees.

Beech tree roots

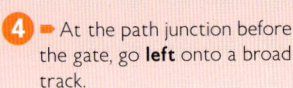

❹ ▸ At the path junction before the gate, go **left** onto a broad track.
▸ Climb gently into woodland and continue to a pond on your right. Here you enter the deer park through the gate ahead.

❺ ▸ Follow the track left to climb between fences and continue up to a T-junction; here turn **right**.
▸ Keep **forward**, later reaching a gate. Shortly beyond it, the path leads to a T-junction with a broad track.

Above: fallow deer
Below: lesser celandine

Top: beech tree leaves
Above: bluebells
Below: wood anemones

The Rookery

Park

wr Park

2 miles

Newton House

6 ➤ Turn **right** to drop past Newton House and the NT café and return to the car park.

Magpie

Walk 1 Dinefwr Park

WALK 2

WATERFALLS WALK

Although best known for its mountain ranges, the Bannau Brycheiniog/Brecon Beacons National Park is also home to some of Wales's most impressive waterfalls, and few places in the country can boast as many fine cascades so close together. This is a stunning walk that visits the spectacular falls of Sgŵd Clun-gwyn and Sgŵd yr Eira. The latter is the real highlight, and a confident walker, who doesn't mind getting wet, can actually follow a path behind the thundering curtain of water (boots needed).

OS information

SN 928124
Explorer OL12

Distance
3.8 miles/6.1 km

Time
3 hours

Start/Finish
Cwm Porth

Parking CF44 9JF
Cwm Porth (Waterfall Country) car park, 1 mile south of Ystradfellte

Public toilets
In car park

Cafés/pubs
Picnic benches at 🚶 and above Sgŵd yr Eira ❺. Snack kiosk in car park, and occasional burger van. Nearest pub: The New Inn, Ystradfellte, CF44 9JE

Terrain
Well-surfaced tracks, but rocky paths and steep steps to both waterfalls

Hilliness
Mostly quite level, but with steep drops to waterfalls; one short ascent on a good path after ⑥

Footwear
Year round

Public transport
None

Did you know? The 'Fforest' in Fforest Fawr, doesn't actually refer to a wood but to a historic hunting estate, once known, in English, as the Great Forest. *Ff* in Welsh is pronounced as an *F* in English, whereas a single *F* is pronounced as a *V*.

Local legend This area of the Brecon Beacons is often linked to King Arthur, who is said to have chased the legendary boar, Twrch Trwyth, through the nearby Mynydd Du mountain range, and is also said to be buried at Dinas Rock, just a few miles from Sgŵd yr Eira. It is easy to imagine the legendary figure crossing the path behind the atmospheric falls.

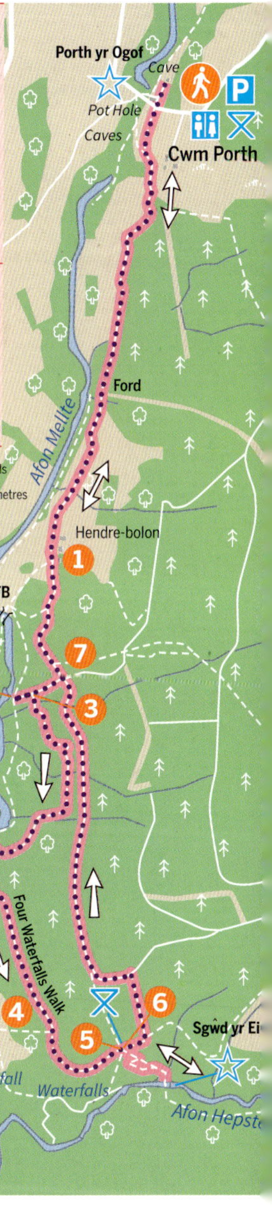

Accessibility
Main path is accessible for powered wheelchairs and for pushchairs; the short, steep paths to the waterfalls are not (see profile)

Dogs
A good dog walk, but care needed around steep ground and fast-flowing rivers. No stiles

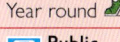

Walk 2 Waterfalls Walk 21

STORIES BEHIND THE WALK

☆ **Waterfalls** As well as being spectacular to look at, the falls encountered on this walk are a wonderful lesson in geology. They are the result of a geological fault that pushed the hard old red sandstone – which makes up the backbone of most of the national park – up against much softer shales. The power of the rivers, which rise high in the mountains, has eroded these shales, leaving shelves of the harder rock exposed. These shelves are clearly visible on most of the waterfalls.

☆ **Porth yr Ogof** While this walk is all about waterfalls, directly beneath the car park at Cwm Porth is an impressive cave entrance: Porth yr Ogof (literally, 'Door of the Cave'). The main entrance, which is easily reached from the car park, is the largest cave entrance in Wales. At one time Porth yr Ogof was used as a showcave.

 Porth yr Ogof
Cwm Porth
Hendre-bolon
½ mile
Sizea crossro

- Walk towards the hut at the car park entrance and go past the barriers to the left of it.
- **Cross** the road and follow the broad, well-surfaced path **ahead** through a succession of gates to a fork in ¾ mile.

❶ - Bear **left** and shortly bend right with the path into woodland.
- Continue to the main crossways with a large waymark and turn **right**, signed 'Sgŵd Clun-gwyn 2 minutes'.

☆ Fforest Fawr

The mountains that give birth to the Afon Mellte and Afon Hepste are part of a massif known as Fforest Fawr, which is one of four main mountain ranges that make up the Brecon Beacons. The highest point of the range is the 2,408-foot Fan Fawr, the southern flanks of which drain into the Afon Hepste, the tumbling river that later produces that imposing curtain of water at Sgŵd yr Eira.

☆ Cave exploration

The Brecon Beacons hide some of Europe's longest and most significant cave systems, and thus have become a mecca for cavers. The caves, which are formed by the action of fast-flowing rivers on the underlying carboniferous limestone, have been extensively explored and mapped and although most are the domain of experienced cavers, the National Showcaves Centre for Wales at Dan yr Ogof (SA9 1GJ; showcaves.co.uk) provides more general access to some spectacular underground scenery.

☆ Sgŵd Clun-gwyn

2 ▸ At the next signposted junction, drop to the fence above the falls then bear **left**, down a pitched path, for a good view of the falls. *Take care!*
▸ Return towards the junction where you first met the fence.

3 ▸ Immediately below the junction, turn **right** onto a clear, rougher path.
▸ Follow the red arrows of the Four Waterfalls Walk through the forest to an interpretation sign at a fork in ⅔ mile.

NATURE NOTES

The western side of the Bannau Brycheiniog/Brecon Beacons National Park, which includes the mountains that feed Waterfall Country, has been declared a UNESCO Global Geopark, in recognition of the value of this amazing landscape.

The rivers that tumble down to and run through Waterfall Country are home to many species of fish, including salmon, and brown and rainbow trout. The rivers provide habitat for fascinating river birds such as dippers — which resemble small blackbirds with a white chest, and which actually walk underwater — and grey wagtails — pretty yellow and grey birds, easily identified by their constantly wagging tails.

Kingfishers can be seen hunting in the calmer pools of the river, although are most often spotted as a blur of neon-like blue.

The woodland is a mix of deciduous trees, such as oak, and plantations of faster-growing evergreens, such as imported Sitka spruce.

Four Waterfalls Walk

Sgŵd yr Eira

2 miles

Afon Hepste

2½ miles

4 ▶ Continue **forwards** here (signed Sgŵd yr Eira) until you reach some benches and another sign, above Sgŵd yr Eira in about 350 yards.

5 ▶ Drop steeply down steps to the riverbank. Here you can scramble over slippery, awkward rocks to walk behind the falls, *but only if you have boots and a waterproof.*

▶ Afterwards, climb steeply back up the steps to the benches.

24 Short Walks Made Easy

Top left: grey wagtail
Above: salmon
Top right: kingfisher
Opposite: oak tree

White-throated dipper

Porth yr Ogof

3 miles

3½ miles   Cwm Porth

6 ▶ Turn **right**, signed Gwaun Hepste; in 75 yards go **left**, uphill on a gravel path to a junction at the top.
▶ Turn **left** (still signed Gwaun Hepste) and continue round the hillside following red arrows for ½ mile, returning to the significant crossroads met earlier.

7 ▶ This time keep **straight ahead**, signed Cwm Porth, and then simply retrace your outward route back to the car park.

This page (clockwise): Canadian War Memorial, Blaen-y-Glyn; Llangattock escarpment; Sugar Loaf from Mynydd Illtud; River Wye
Opposite (clockwise): Newton House, Dinefwr; Monmouthshire and Brecon Canal; Sgŵd Clun-gwyn waterfall

WALK 3

MYNYDD ILLTUD

There's something wonderful about a relatively level walk that offers great mountain views, and this is one of the best. It starts at the popular Mountain Centre, on Mynydd Illtud Common, where there are some interesting displays and a welcome café. It then crosses the common to visit the lofty remnants of an Iron Age fort, all the time offering spectacular high-peak views. The going is wonderful underfoot, and the return leg visits a ruined chapel.

OS information

SN 978263
Explorer OL12

Distance
4.25 miles/6.8km

Time
2¼ hours

Start/Finish
Bannau Brycheiniog/
Brecon Beacons
National Park Visitor
Centre

Parking LD3 8ER
Visitor Centre car
park, near Libanus

Public toilets
In Visitor Centre

Cafés/pubs
Caffi y Fan in the
Visitor Centre

Terrain
Mostly grassy paths;
lanes

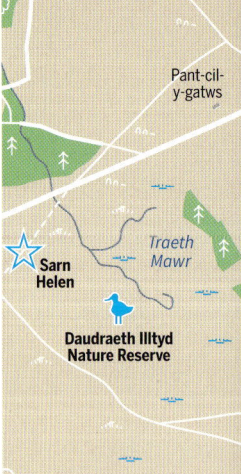

28 Short Walks Made Easy

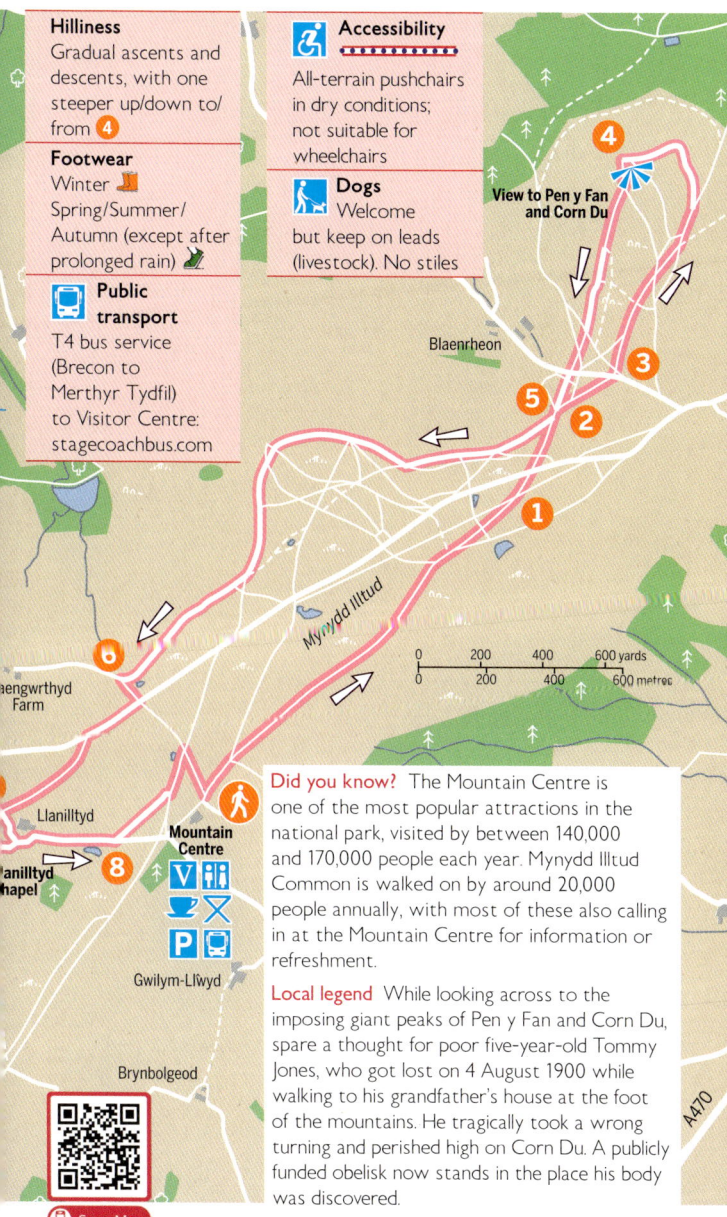

STORIES BEHIND THE WALK

+ Llanilltyd Chapel This chapel lies on the edge of Mynydd Illtud Common, just a short walk from the Mountain Centre. There's not much left of the actual building beyond foundations, but the compound still has its graves and headstones. It's named after Saint Illtyd, and legend suggests it's the site where the 5th-century saint was martyred and then buried. The chapel dates back to at least the 14th century, possibly older.

Visitor Centre (Mountain Centre)

Often referred to as simply the Mountain Centre, the National Park Visitor Centre is a wonderful place to visit, with a shop, an excellent café and an information centre with informative displays and great staff. There are also public toilets, a children's play area and a large car park that is perfect for this walk.

- Leave by the gate at the bottom of the car park and take the **right-hand** grassy track of the two leading straight ahead. Immediately fork **right** again on another grassy track, walking to a crossways of tracks in ¾ mile.

1 - Turn **left**, now on a fainter grassy track and follow it to the lane.
- Walk **straight across** onto a clear track rising over the brow of the hill to reach a fence corner and metal field gate, on the left.

2 - Here, fork **right** and drop to a lane in a dip.
- **Cross** the road and follow the clear track **ahead**.

☆ Bannau Brycheiniog/ Brecon Beacons National Park

The national park was one of ten set up in Britain in the 1950s to conserve the scenery, culture and landscape of some of the country's most beautiful places. Covering 519 square miles, it stretches from Llandeilo in the west to Abergavenny in the east, and from Hay-on-Wye in the north to Merthyr Tydfil in the south. It is run by the National Park Authority whose job it is to balance the needs of the landscape and environment with the demands of both visitors and local people.

☆ Sarn Helen

Running through Mynydd Illtud, close to Llanilltyd Chapel, is a Roman road – Sarn Helen. The road originally connected the north Welsh coast at Aberconwy with the south, in Carmarthenshire, totalling over 160 miles in length. It is thought to have been named after Saint Elen of Caernarfon, a Celtic saint whose story is told in *The Mabinogion*. However, another theory suggests it refers to the mistress of a Roman commander.

3 ▶ This leads up and to the right towards a wall.
▶ Follow the wall (right) for 150 yards then fork **left** to the shoulder of Twyn yr Gaer.
▶ At the highest point, turn **left** to walk easily to the summit trig point.

4 ▶ With your back to the trig pillar and a view to Pen y Fan and Corn Du dominating the horizon, take the broad grassy track descending directly into the valley ahead, **cross** the lane and aim for the fence corner/metal gate met earlier **2**.

Walk 3 Mynydd Illtud

NATURE NOTES

The common land south-west of the Mountain Centre holds two boggy pools: Traeth Mawr and Traeth Bach, which form the main part of the Illtyd Pools Site of Special Scientific Interest (SSSI). To the untrained eye, the area may appear as a large boggy plateau, but the underlying geology of the two wetlands are actually quite distinct and host different vegetation, including rare sedges, sphagnum mosses and spiders. They attract wintering flocks of teal, a small, colourful duck.

The common itself is covered with bracken, which is actually harvested for animal bedding. You're almost bound to spot skylarks, stonechats and wheatears, which are small, light-coloured birds with a distinct white rump. Often, masters of the air currents overhead, you'll see beautiful red kites, raptors easily identified by their forked tails.

If you're eating or drinking in Caffi y Fan, your crumbs will be eagerly sought by bold little chaffinches – the males have a lovely pink face and breast.

Bracken bales

5 ▶ Now, simply keep the wall/fence on your right and follow the track round the perimeter of the common.
▶ After just over 1 mile, pass a small pond and soon after meet a gravel farm track.

6 ▶ Go **left** to meet the lane, **cross** over and in a few paces turn **right** to follow a grassy track parallel to the lane to a fork in 200 yards.
▶ Fork **left** and climb gently to another road.

Traeth Mawr

Top left: chaffinch
Top right: common teal
Above: wheatear

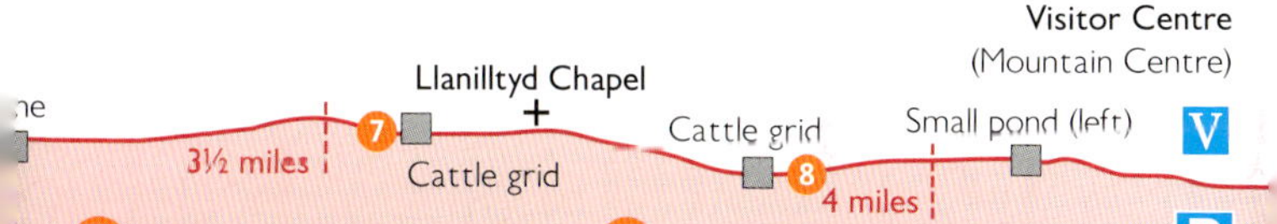

7 ▶ Turn **left**, over the cattle grid. Just past the farmhouse, to visit Llanilltyd Chapel ruin, go through a gate on the right, then through the right-hand of two gates ahead.
▶ After visiting, go **right** along the lane for 350 yards to a cattle grid.

8 ▶ Fork **left** and follow a grassy track up and over a small rise.
▶ As the fence bends away to the left, keep **forward** to a grassy track intersection near a small pond and turn **right** to return to the Mountain Centre.

Walk 3 Mynydd Illtud

WALK 4

BRECON CANAL BASIN AND RIVER USK

The small market town of Brecon lies on the northern boundary of the national park and is blessed with stunning views southwards towards the park's highest peaks. It's one of the main centres in the national park and a great base for walking. This route takes a level, easy-going loop around the town's two main waterways – the River Usk and the Monmouthshire and Brecon Canal. As well as exploring some lovely countryside, it also touches on the area's industrial past.

OS information
SO 045281 Explorer OL12
Distance 3.9 miles / 6.3 km
Time 2 hours
Start/Finish Theatr Brycheiniog, Brecon
Parking LD3 7HL Brycheiniog car park
Public toilets Theatr Brycheiniog
Cafés/pubs The Waterfront Café in Theatr Brycheiniog; many other options in Brecon
Terrain Well-surfaced canal towpath; grassy field paths (muddy in very wet weather)

34 Short Walks Made Easy

Hilliness
Level throughout

Footwear
Year round (boots in very wet weather)

Public transport
Bus services to Brecon: traveline.cymru

Accessibility
Wheelchair and pushchair friendly along canal towpath, ① to ③

Dogs
Welcome, but keep on leads around livestock. No stiles

Did you know? Brecon was the base for the South Wales Borderers, also known as the 24th Regiment, who fought the Zulus in the battles of Isandlwana and Rorke's Drift in the late 1800s. Isandlwana proved disastrous for the British troops, who were terribly outnumbered and suffered great losses. But their heroic stand at Rorke's Drift became legendary and was dramatised in the 1964 film, *Zulu*. In 1969, the regiment became part of the Royal Regiment of Wales.

Local legend Brecon was the birthplace of actress Sarah Siddons (1755–1831), who is recognised as one of the leading tragedy actresses of the 18th century. She was best known for her portrayal of Shakespeare's Lady Macbeth and was once described as 'tragedy personified.' The Sarah Siddons Society was formed in her honour in 1952 and still presents the annual Sarah Siddons Award to distinguished actresses.

Walk 4 Brecon Canal Basin and River Usk

STORIES BEHIND THE WALK

☆ **Brecon** Named after a 5th-century Welsh prince, Brychan (Brycheiniog in Welsh), the town of Brecon grew up around the confluence of the Afon Honddu and River Usk (the Welsh name, Aberhonddu, refers to this, with Aber meaning confluence). It hosts the ruins of an 11th-century castle and an eye-catching cathedral. The town has a population of around 10,000 people and is famous for an annual jazz festival as well as for its nearby mountains.

🏠 **Theatr Brycheiniog**
This walk starts alongside the impressive, brick-built Theatr Brycheiniog, which was opened in April 1997, and is famous for being the first wholly National Lottery-funded new-build arts organisation in Great Britain. It seats 477 people in the main auditorium, with a smaller 120-seat rehearsal studio also available, and runs a busy programme of events including theatre, dance and music.

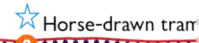
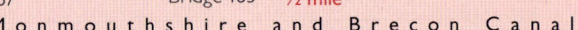

Monmouthshire and Brecon Canal

➤ From the car park, **cross** to the canal basin, keeping Theatr Brycheiniog on your right.
➤ Take the ramp down to the towpath, pass under bridge 167 and walk with the canal on your left for ½ mile to a fork 200 yards beyond bridge 165.

❶ ➤ Branch **right** to continue along the lane to see Watton Limekilns.
➤ Return to the fork and turn sharp **right** to follow the canal to the wonderful wooden sculpture depicting a coal miner with a horse-drawn tram.

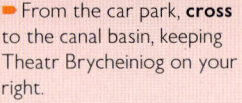
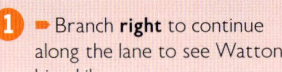

36 Short Walks Made Easy

⭐ **Watton Limekilns** Beneath Watton Wharf lie the Watton Limekilns. These impressive structures were originally built in the early 1800s and used to produce quicklime for building and agriculture. The tops of the kilns are level with the canal so they could be loaded easily directly from boats, and the lane below, which you will walk along, was constructed to remove the finished product. In all, the process took around seven days. The kilns were restored in 2022.

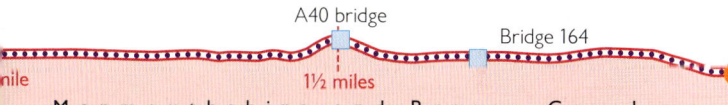

A40 bridge — 1½ miles — Bridge 164

Monmouthshire and Brecon Canal

② ▶ **Continue** beside the canal, later passing beneath the A40.
▶ ¼ mile beyond bridge 164, keep an eye open for a path leading to a gate on the right.

③ ▶ Drop sharp **right** to go through the gate and follow the path through fields with the River Usk to your left.
▶ Continue over a footbridge and through a small gate to reach a metal field gate, with the A40 ahead.

Walk 4 Brecon Canal Basin and River Usk 37

NATURE NOTES

Canals are wonderful places to enjoy nature, with the still or slow-flowing waters supporting many species. The most common fish along the waterway are roach, dace, chub, perch and eels. Among the common birds you're likely to see along this stretch are mallards and moorhens. The striking red patch at the top of a moorhen's beak is an indication to other moorhens of a bird's health – the brighter the patch, the fitter the individual.

Plant life abounds – particularly fine are the flowers of yellow flag iris. Also known as water flag, the handsome yellow flowers may be seen in late spring and early summer, with plants standing up to 5 feet tall.

Look out for butterflies too, especially the black, red and white of the red admiral. Like small tortoiseshell and peacock butterflies, red admiral caterpillars feed on stinging nettle, a valuable plant for wildlife.

On the River Usk, keep your eyes peeled for goosanders – colourful diving ducks.

Top: red admiral butterfly
Above: red admiral caterpillars

4 ▸ Pass through the gate and under the main road and stay beside the Usk for 1 mile to a waymarked footpath on the right (this comes about ⅓ mile after the path to the water treatment plant).

5 ▸ Go **right**, leaving the river behind. The path soon becomes a clear track leading past the rugby club and back to the canal.
▸ Here turn **left**, back along the towpath to Theatr Brycheiniog.

38 Short Walks Made Easy

Goosander

Above: moorhen
Below: yellow flag iris

Rugby Club Bridge 165 Bridge 166 Theatr Brycheiniog

3 miles   3½ miles   Bridge 167

Monmouthshire and Brecon Canal

☆ Horse-drawn tram

The horse-drawn tram sculpture seen on this walk harks back to the Watton Wharf terminus of the Hay Railway, a horse-drawn tramway that, in 1820, connected Brecon with Kington in Herefordshire, a distance of over 36 miles, making it the world's longest tramway of its type. It was later converted to run steam trains. The line was used solely for carrying goods including coal, limestone and lime, food, drink and farm produce.

Opposite (clockwise): red kite; fallow deer; celandines and wood anemones
This page (clockwise): heron; grey squirrel; teal; foxgloves

WALK 5

BLAEN-Y-GLYN

The stunning Afon Caerfanell rises on a boggy upland plateau, close to the highest mountains in the national park, and tumbles down a steep escarpment into a beautiful wild valley, where it joins forces with the Nant Blaen-y-glyn. The combined waters race southwards, plummeting over the sizeable waterfall that's visited on this walk. The river continues its breakneck pace downstream providing spectacle throughout the return leg. It may be short, but it's one of the finest walks in the national park.

OS information

SO 062170
Explorer OL12

Distance
1 mile/1.6km

Time
½ hour

Start/Finish
Blaen-y-glyn Isaf

Parking CF48 2UT
Blaen-y-glyn Isaf car park

Public toilets
None (nearest at Talybont-on-Usk)

Cafés/pubs
None (nearest café – Old Barn Tearoom, Torpantau, CF48 2UT; nearest pub – White Hart, Talybont-on-Usk)

Terrain
Rough, rocky tracks with some muddy sections

Hilliness
Steady climb outbound and steady descent on the return, with a couple of steep up-and-down ramps

Footwear
Winter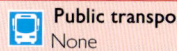
Spring/Summer/Autumn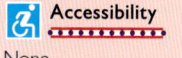

Public transport
None

Accessibility
••••••••••
None

Dogs
Welcome, but keep on lead around livestock. No stiles

Did you know? During colder winters, the Caerfanell Waterfall will freeze completely and becomes a much-coveted ice climb. Climbing enthusiasts will travel from miles around to ascend the steep ice fall with the aid of crampons (spikes attached to their boots), and the use of two small ice axes. It's hard to imagine this scene when you view the falls in full spate in summer.

Local legend Welsh international forward, Fred Miller, was born in Talybont-on-Usk in 1873. He played club rugby for Mountain Ash and was called up for his country to face the Irish in 1896. He later moved to northern England and continued his career playing Rugby League.

STORIES BEHIND THE WALK

☆ **Natural Resources Wales** The Blaen-y-Glyn Isaf car park, where this walk begins, and the surrounding forestry is owned and managed by Natural Resources Wales, a government-sponsored body formed in 2013 by the amalgamation of Forestry Commission Wales, the Countryside Council for Wales and the Environment Agency for Wales. The organisation's remit is to 'pursue sustainable management of natural resources' in Wales.

☆ **Canadian War Memorial** High above the falls, close to the source of the Afon Caerfanell and Nant Blaen-y-glyn, is a touching memorial to the crew of flight R1465, a Canadian bomber, struck down in bad weather on a routine training flight on 6 July 1942. A plaque on the memorial lists the names of those who lost their lives and the wreckage of the plane still peppers the hillside. It's a moving spot, high on Waun Rydd, but only reached by quite a strenuous walk.

Blaen-y-glyn

Blaen-y-glyn Isaf

■ Leave the car park by going past the barrier at its far end.
■ Climb steadily on the rocky track, with the river below to the right.

■ In ⅓ mile, cross a concrete bridge. Here a lesser path leads off left to a series of small cascades, which are worth a detour if you have the time and energy.
■ Continue on the main track to a fork 50 yards further on.

⭐ Pont Blaen-y-glyn

The stone bridge crossed at the end of this walk is known as Pont Blaen-y-glyn and is a Grade II-listed structure. It was most likely built in the 1800s as roads were developed to connect the Monmouthshire and Brecon Canal, which passes through nearby Talybont-on-Usk, to the South Wales valleys. The canal between here and Brecon opened in 1800. Pont means bridge in Welsh and a crossing here almost certainly dates back to the Roman occupation.

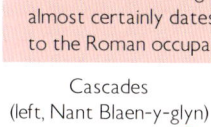

① ▸ The main waterfall is signed down to the **right**.
▸ Descend to a kissing-gate and continue down to a footbridge, where the waterfall is now on the left.

② ▸ The way back lies over the footbridge and then **right**; but, first, it is well worth getting a closer look at the falls, which can be gained from using either bank – *take good care as it can be slippery.*
▸ After crossing the footbridge, you can rise to the fingerpost and detour **left** up above the falls to enjoy more cascades and some fine rocky viewpoints. Return to the footbridge.

Walk 5 Blaen-y-glyn

NATURE NOTES

One of the loudest songsters in the valley must be the tiny wren whose piercing warbling is often surprising considering it's such a diminutive bird. Wrens seem to thrive in upland environments, where they often nest in drystone walls. Pied flycatchers can also be seen in summer. About the size of a sparrow, pied flycatchers are summer visitors, migrating from West Africa.

The drystone walls also play host to some wonderful mosses and lichens, which seem to almost glow green on a bright morning.

In May, the valley is dotted with flowering hawthorn that produces fine spring blossom. Hawthorn is known by several other names including whitethorn, quickthorn and, most commonly, May, after the month in which it blooms. Look out for foxgloves swaying in the breeze, adding colour to the scene.

The track up to the falls can also be a good place to see toads, which can cross the road in large numbers, usually at night, during their spring and autumn migrations.

Male and female pied flycatcher

Footbridge

½ mile

Blaen-y-glyn

3 ► This time keep **ahead**, with the river and its tumbling rapids and small cascades to your right.

► Follow the path, which is uneven and steep in places, all the way down to a gate beside Pont Blaen-y-glyn.

4 ► Go through the gate and turn **right** onto the road to cross the bridge.

► The car park is on the **right**.

Moss-covered drystone wall

Speckled wood butterfly on hawthorn blossom

Above: common toad
Below: wren

Pont Blaen-y-glyn ☆　　　1 mile

④

Blaen-y-glyn Isaf

☆ Talybont Reservoir

Close to the start of this walk lies the magnificent Talybont Reservoir (car park at LD3 7YS), a huge expanse of water formed by the damming of the Afon Caerfanell to provide drinking water to Newport. Construction of the current dam began in 1931 after an earlier treatment plant had failed, and the first drinking water was supplied to Newport in 1939.

Walk 5 Blaen-y-glyn

WALK 6

BRYNICH LOCK TO TALYBONT-ON-USK

Linked at both ends by a regular bus service, this easy-going and level walk provides a wonderful day out in glorious scenery. As well as great views, you have a chance to see a working lock at the start, there's abundant wildlife both on and off the water, and also an opportunity for refreshments in a fine local pub at half distance. It also requires minimum route finding as it follows the canal towpath for its entire length.

OS information
SO 077273 Explorer OL13
Distance 4.9 miles/7.9 km
Time 2½ hours
Start Brynich Lock **Finish** Talybont-on-Usk
Parking LD3 7YQ The Hub, Penpentre, Talybont-on-Usk
Public toilets The Hub
Cafés/pubs Café in Talybont Stores. White Hart Inn and Star Inn in Talybont-on-Usk. Royal Oak at Pencelli (halfway along)
Terrain Well-surfaced canal towpath throughout
Hilliness Level throughout
Footwear Year round 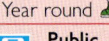
Public transport Bus service 43 between Brecon and Abergavenny links Talybont-on-Usk with Brynich Lock: stagecoachbus.com (Bus stop outside White Hart in Talybont)

48 Short Walks Made Easy

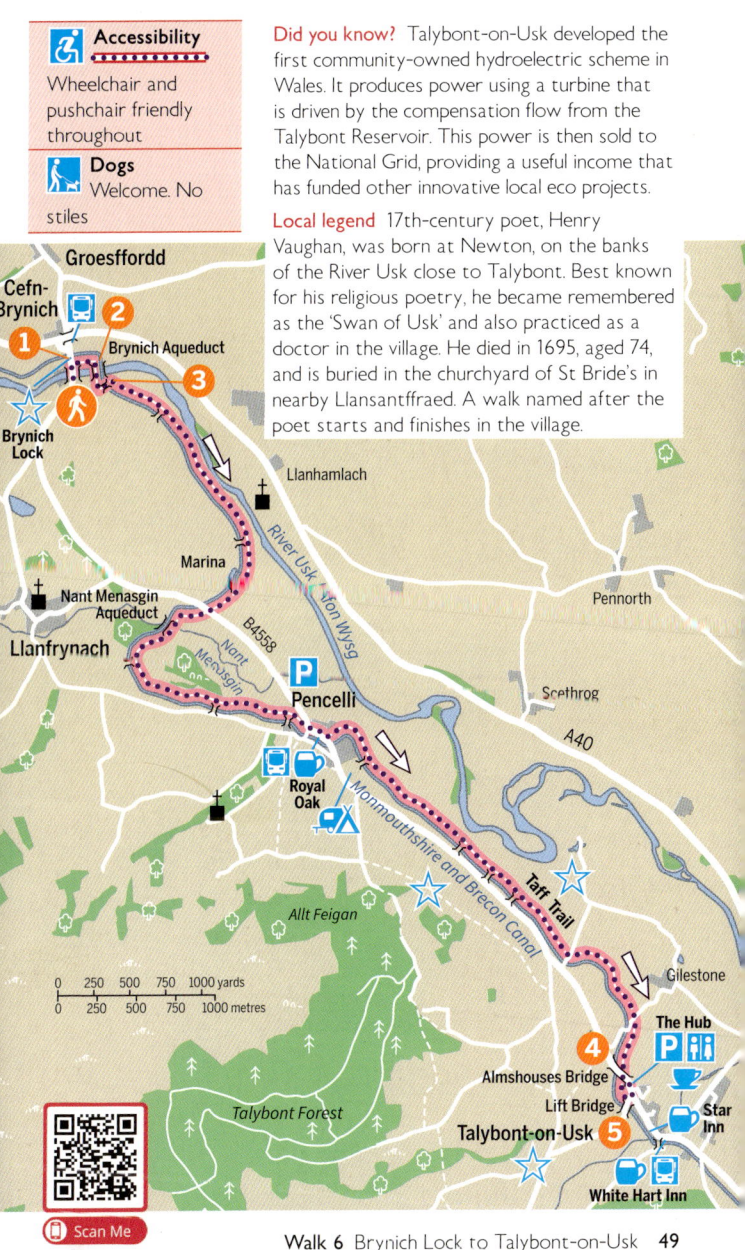

Did you know? Talybont-on-Usk developed the first community-owned hydroelectric scheme in Wales. It produces power using a turbine that is driven by the compensation flow from the Talybont Reservoir. This power is then sold to the National Grid, providing a useful income that has funded other innovative local eco projects.

Local legend 17th-century poet, Henry Vaughan, was born at Newton, on the banks of the River Usk close to Talybont. Best known for his religious poetry, he became remembered as the 'Swan of Usk' and also practiced as a doctor in the village. He died in 1695, aged 74, and is buried in the churchyard of St Bride's in nearby Llansantffraed. A walk named after the poet starts and finishes in the village.

Accessibility Wheelchair and pushchair friendly throughout

Dogs Welcome. No stiles

Walk 6 Brynich Lock to Talybont-on-Usk 49

STORIES BEHIND THE WALK

☆ **Taff Trail** This section of canal towpath also forms a length of the 55-mile-long Taff Trail that runs between Brecon and Cardiff. The trail leaves the canal at Talybont-on-Usk and takes the line of an old railway west, over the hills, to join the Taff Valley, which it then follows south through Merthyr Tydfil and on to the capital.

☆ **Talybont-on-Usk**

This small village sits between the River Usk and the Monmouthshire and Brecon Canal and makes a great base for walking, with a well-stocked shop, a café and three pubs.

Brynich Lock

Brynich Aqueduct (River Usk)
 ½ mile

Taff Trail

☆ Monmouthshire an 1 mile

▶ From the bus stop, walk **downhill** to visit Brynich Lock, accessed via the gate on your **right**.

▶ Leave the lock by **crossing** the road and passing through the gate **ahead** onto the towpath, canal to your left.

① ▶ Now continue easily to the Brynich Aqueduct in about 175 yards.

50 Short Walks Made Easy

Brynich Lock

The lock at Brynich was created at the same time as the canal and was first operational around 1800. The canal south of the Brynich Aqueduct, which is crossed on this walk, is slightly lower than the section that leads on to the Canal Basin in Brecon, so boats are lowered or raised here via this excellent example of what is termed a pound lock.

1½ miles | Aqueduct (Nant Menasgin)
Marina (right) | 2 miles

recon Canal

2 ▪ **Cross** the aqueduct and continue to a ramp that leads to a gate and a bridge over the canal in 200 yards.
▪ Turn **left** to cross the canal, and then **right** to join the towpath on the other side.

3 ▪ Continue with the canal on your right for 2½ miles to reach the Royal Oak pub at Pencelli.
▪ Continue along the towpath for another 2 miles to reach a fork on the outskirts of Talybont-on-Usk.

NATURE NOTES

Along the canal banks in spring, domesticated plants, such as daffodils, stand among wildflowers like primroses and bluebells.

You have a good chance of seeing a heron along this peaceful waterway. The canal is a hunting ground for them as they stalk small amphibians, fish, worms or even small birds. You may also hear the drumming of a great spotted woodpecker. These handsome black and white birds, with red underparts, nest in the towering trees that line the canal banks.

Some of the mature trees have bracket fungi, also called polypore or shelf fungi. Beefsteak fungi grow on dead or dying oaks; birch polypore may be found on dead or dying birch trees; and turkey tail, with its multiple fan-shaped brackets, favours fallen deciduous timber.

The River Usk has a resident population of otters, so if you go quietly and are walking the towpath in early morning or late evening, you may be lucky enough to spot one. The sluggish waters of the canal are home to great crested newts, Britain's largest newt species.

Otter

2½ miles — Royal Oak, Pencelli

Taff Trail — 3 miles — 3½ miles

☆ Monmouthshire and Brecon Canal

4 ▶ Bear **right** to keep beside the canal for 300 yards to meet a lift bridge in Talybont.

5 ▶ Bear **left** to drop to the road.
▶ Bear **left** again and walk along the pavement to return to the Hub car park (next right).

Great spotted woodpecker

Beefsteak fungus

Above: turkey tail
Below: birch polypore

4 miles — Almshouses Bridge — 4½ miles — ④ — Lift Bridge — ⑤ — Talybont-on-Usk

The Hub

☆ **Monmouthshire and Brecon Canal** The canal was originally two adjoining canals: the Monmouthshire Canal, from Newport to Pontymoile Basin, and the Brecknock and Abergavenny Canal, running from Pontymoile to Brecon. They were constructed to carry coal, iron and limestone and were eventually put out of business by the railways. Both were originally opened around 1800 but eventually abandoned in the early 1960s. Renamed as the Monmouthshire and Brecon Canal, the current canal, which consists mostly of the original Brecknock and Abergavenny Canal, was reopened for leisure use in 1970. The navigable section runs for approximately 36 miles from Brecon to Five Locks, near Cwmbran. It's possible to walk or cycle the whole length.

Walk 6 Brynich Lock to Talybont-on-Usk

WALK 7

CRAIG Y CILAU

This walk could win prizes for the best mountain views possible from an easy-going route. It's fairly level throughout and follows predominantly well-surfaced paths, yet it explores a fascinating limestone landscape, brimming with points of interest, and comes with incredible vistas across the Usk Valley to the Black Mountains. What this remote spot lacks in facilities, it more than makes up for in wildness and wow factor – a true gem.

OS information
SO 209153 Explorer OL13
Distance 2.5 miles/4km
Time 1½ hours
Start/Finish Llangattock Escarpment
Parking NP8 1LG Car park off Hafod Road, about 3 miles south of Crickhowell and 3 miles west of Gilwern
Public toilets None (nearest in Crickhowell)
Cafés/pubs None (nearest in Crickhowell)

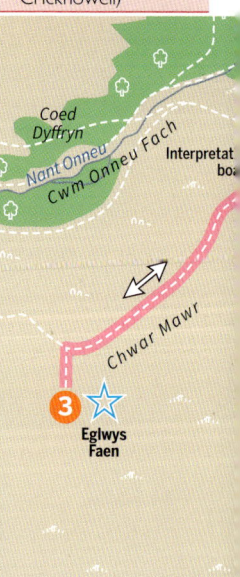

Terrain	Mainly firm tracks, rocky in places
Hilliness	Two short ascents
Footwear	Year round
Public transport	None
Accessibility	to ❷ is tarmac or well-surfaced track and level, making it accessible for wheelchairs and pushchairs
Dogs	Welcome, but keep on leads (livestock). No stiles

Did you know? Concealed on a hillside close to Craig y Cilau is a large fissure in the rock known as Chartist's Cave. The Chartist movement took its name from the People's Charter of 1838 and was a national protest movement, with a strong presence in industrial South Wales. The rebels used the cave to stockpile weapons.

Local legend Just before you reach the caves at Eglwys Faen, you'll see a brass plaque on a rock on the left that reads: In memory of Bill Gascoine, the man that followed the water. The man in question was a much-respected caver, best known for his extensive water-tracing work in the limestone regions of South Wales. His discoveries led to a detailed understanding of the local hydrology and of the major cave systems. He died in 2012, aged 73.

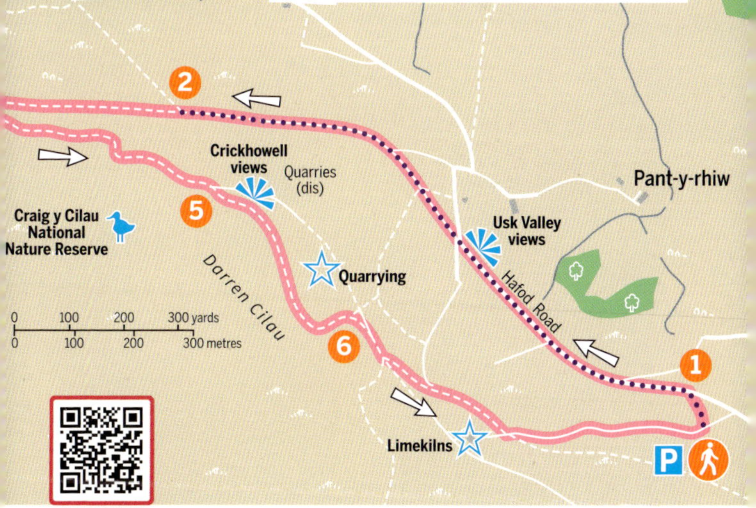

Walk 7 Craig y Cilau

STORIES BEHIND THE WALK

🐦 **Craig y Cilau National Nature Reserve** Perched high above the Usk Valley, the former quarry site of Craig y Cilau was designated a national nature reserve in 1959. Famous for its wide array of alpine plants and trees, some extremely rare, the reserve covers around 157 acres and boasts incredibly varied geology with old red sandstone above the limestone escarpment, visited on this walk, and millstone grit beneath it.

☆ **Crickhowell**
The village of Crickhowell, seen below in the valley for much of this walk, is an excellent place to stop off for food or drink. Built on the banks of the River Usk and close to the Monmouthshire and Brecon Canal, the town takes its name from the Welsh, Crug Hywel, which is an Iron Age fort above the town, often referred to as Table Mountain.

Usk Valley views

½ mile

P Llangattock Escarpment car park

Craig y Cilau Nationa

① ▶ Turn **left** along the lane. In ⅓ mile, keep **forward** below houses, soon arriving at open ground.
▶ Keep **straight ahead** and walk easily round the hillside for ¼ mile, to reach a large block of stone, where the path narrows.

▶ Walk back out of the car park and start down the access track before forking **left** onto a grassy cut-through that leads to the road below.

Short Walks Made Easy

☆ Quarrying

In the late 19th century, the cliffs you see on the walk were quarried for limestone, which was then used in iron-making. Some of the limestone was hauled by horse-drawn tramway – the route of which is now the road this walk starts on – to the ironworks at Brynmawr, and some would have been dropped by a series of inclines to the Monmouthshire and Brecon Canal at Llangattock.

☆ Eglwys Faen

The caves of Eglwys Faen make a great focal point for this walk. The name literally translates to Church of Stone and it is thought that the caves may have been used as a hiding place during times of religious persecution. There are many entrances, some of which are accessible. You can peer in, *but be careful and stay within the day-lit confines as the darkness masks a very uneven floor and some steep drops.*

2 ▶ Follow this spectacularly located narrow path for ¼ mile until you meet another narrow path dropping in from the left – this is your return route.
▶ For now, keep **ahead**, past an interpretation board, and continue to an open area in another ¼ mile, where you'll see small cave openings in the cliffs to your left. This is Eglwys Faen.

Walk 7 Craig y Cilau 57

NATURE NOTES

The cliffs of Craig y Cilau are composed of carboniferous limestone, a hard sedimentary rock that was formed at the bottom of shallow tropical seas from the shells of millions of sea creatures encased in mud. It's a highly soluble rock; hence the vast network of caves that penetrate deep into the hillside. The caves themselves support a population of lesser horseshoe bats – a protected species found only in the west of the British Isles.

Rue-leaved saxifrage is one of a number of rare alpine plants found at Craig y Cilau. More than 250 wildflower species have been recorded here too.

The cliffs are a prime nesting site for ravens, the largest member of the crow family. This is a great place to spot the ring ouzel, or mountain blackbird as it's often called, and green woodpeckers are common on the open hillside – their 'yaffle' call giving them away, often making them heard before they're seen.

Among the trees found here are species of whitebeam. The underneath of whitebeam leaves are covered in characteristic felt-like white hair. Clusters of scarlet berries develop in late summer.

Rue-leaved saxifrage

3 ▶ After enjoying the site, return to the interpretation board noted previously.

4 ▶ Fork **right**, uphill. There are a few paths here but stick with the main one, winding your way gently upward for ⅓ mile to a fork, with the cliffs up to your right. The path joins a broader grassy track before the way splits.

Top: green woodpecker
Bottom: whitebeam

Top: ring ouzel Middle: raven
Bottom: lesser horseshoe bat

Crickhowell
views ☆ Quarrying
2 miles ⑥

Path to limekilns (right)

Llangattock Escarpment car park

2½ miles P

en Cilau

ature Reserve

⑤ ▶ Bear **right** at the fork to walk towards the cliffs. Then go **left** to walk parallel to them.

▶ At a cairn, turn **left** onto another broad track. Follow this between raised banks and round to the right.

⑥ ▶ By a concrete bunker, keep **left** at a fork to stay with the lower path.

▶ At the path junction in ¼ mile, a short detour **right** leads to some old limekilns.

▶ To return to the car park, turn **left** (**right** if you've visited the limekilns) and easily follow the clear track downhill back to the start.

Walk 7 Craig y Cilau 59

Opposite (clockwise): Caffi y Fan, Mynydd Illtud; Royal Oak, Pencelli; The Coffee Pot, Abergavenny
This page (clockwise): Brecon Farmers Market; Kilverts Inn, Hay-on-Wye; Welsh cakes; Castle Hotel, Brecon; Abergavenny Food Festival

WALK 8

HAY-ON-WYE

Famous for its bookshops and book festival, the vibrant little riverside town of Hay-on-Wye also makes a great base for exploring the Brecon Beacons. Hay sits on the banks of the meandering River Wye, and this 2-mile walk traces the riverbanks for much of its fine and level route. It's a lovely walk that transports you from the bustling streets of the town to the tranquillity of the Warren — a colourful riverside meadow — and then back again via a disused railway.

OS information
SO 229427
Explorer OL13

Distance
2.1 miles/3.4km

Time
1¼ hours

Start/Finish
Hay-on-Wye

Parking HR3 5BJ
Wyeford car park, Wyeford Road

Public toilets
Canolfan Hay Craft Centre

Cafés/pubs
Hay-on-Wye

Terrain
Well-surfaced paths and grassy riverbank

Hilliness
Level or gently undulating, with a short rise from ❷ and from ❸ to ❹

Footwear
Year round

Public transport
Hay-on-Wye is on the T14 bus service between Hereford and Brecon: stagecoachbus.com (Hereford is the nearest railway station with a bus service to Hay)

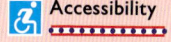
Accessibility
Wheelchair and pushchair friendly to ① and ④ to end

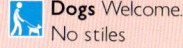
Dogs Welcome. No stiles

Did you know? Despite being in Wales, Hay-on-Wye has a Hereford postcode. The town's Welsh name is Y Gelli Gandryll, which means 'the grove under the rainbow.' The main supermarket, a Co-op, however, is actually in England, so subject to English trading law rather than Welsh.

Local legends On April Fool's Day, 1977, a Hay-on-Wye resident, Richard Booth, conceived a bizarre publicity stunt in which he declared the town to be an 'independent kingdom' with himself as king and his horse, prime minister. Although his independence bid failed, Booth is largely accredited with creating Hay's book-town legacy. He was awarded an MBE in 2004 for his contribution to tourism and died in 2019, aged 80.

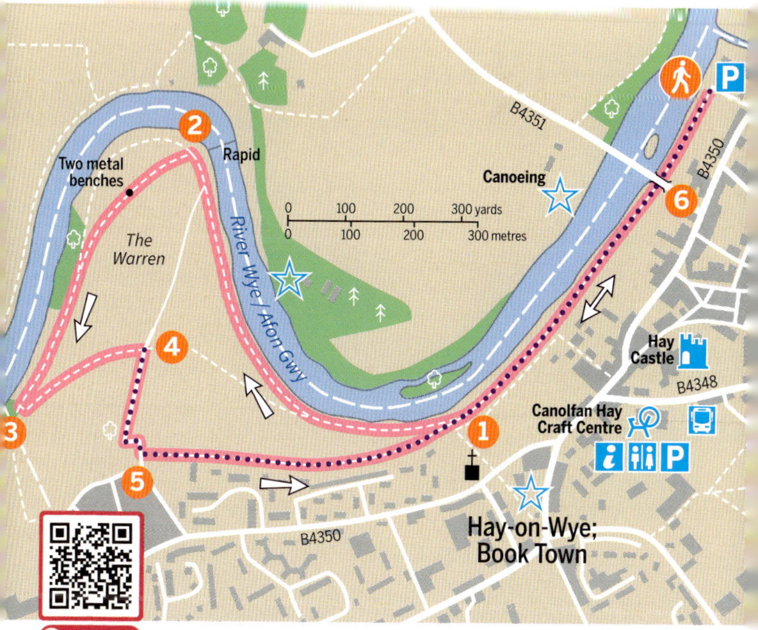

Walk 8 Hay-on-Wye

STORIES BEHIND THE WALK

☆ **Book Town** Hay-on-Wye is most famous for being the world's largest second-hand and antiquarian book centre. The town has over 20 bookshops, including some that are spread over two or more floors. It also hosts an annual book festival, more formally known as the Hay Festival of Literature & Arts, which takes place over 10 days towards the end of May.

☆ **Hay-on-Wye** The town of Hay-on-Wye, or Hay as it's usually known, just squeezes inside the northernmost tip of the Bannau Brycheiniog/Brecon Beacons National Park, north of the Black Mountains and very close to the Wales/England border. It is home to around 2,000 people and boasts over 150 listed buildings. It's a bustling little place with an active theatre and a busy market in the town centre every Thursday.

Hay-on-Wye; Book Town ☆ ☆ Canoeing

☆ River Wye

½ mile

Wyeford car park

- From the car park, facing the river, turn **left** to walk between gateposts and onto the lower of two tracks, following it with the river to your right for about ⅓ mile to a gate.

- Pass through the gateway, the path narrowing here
- Keep **straight ahead** at a junction – signed to the Warren – and continue to a gate marking the Warren's entrance.

64 Short Walks Made Easy

☆ Canoeing
The Wye has over 80 miles of waterway navigable by kayakers and canoeists, making it incredibly popular with enthusiasts. Many outfitters ply their trade in the area and can arrange excursions ranging from short paddles to longer expeditions. There are several campsites along the riverbanks – ideal for waterway-based holidays.

☆ River Wye
The River Wye rises high in the mountains of Mid Wales, just over a mile from the source of Britain's longest river, the River Severn. Interestingly, the Wye sets off eastwards before veering south, travelling its full 156-mile course within Wales, whereas the Severn crosses into England before eventually turning back south and emptying into the Bristol Channel. The two rivers finally meet at Chepstow, close to the Severn Crossings. The Wye is actually Britain's fourth longest river.

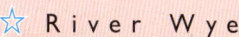

The Warren   Rapid ❷   Metal benches   1 mile

☆ River Wye

❶
- Keep **straight ahead** to a fork and then bear **right** to drop closer to the river.
- Continue with the river to your right, reaching a path junction just before a rapid.

❷
- Turn **uphill**, climbing away from the river on a grassy path leading between two metal benches.
- Keep **ahead**. In 150 yards, walk with a fence to your left, following it for a further 150 yards to reach a waymarked gate.

NATURE NOTES

The riverbanks and adjacent land are home to several species of mammal, including badgers, foxes, rabbits, hedgehogs and even otters, although these can be shy and rather elusive. Look out also for grey squirrels moving acrobatically through the trees.

The meadows of the Warren come alive with colour in spring and cuckooflower, in particular, covers the grassy slopes above the river. Towering over the Wye are some impressive white willow trees and the waters themselves are frequented by grayling — a member of the salmon family, with a long slender body and, for its body size, a large dorsal fin. Go quietly and you may even see a kingfisher.

Top: white willow
Right: cuckooflower

The Warren · 1½ miles
Disused railway path

3 ▪ Pass through the gate and bear **diagonally left** to the corner of the hedge, 100 yards in front.
▪ Keep the hedge to your right and continue on a grassy path to a gate.

4 ▪ Go through the gate and turn **right** onto a straight track.
▪ In 150 yards, pass between steep walls before turning **sharp left**, between posts, to climb onto a disused railway path/cycleway.

Top left: hedgehog
Top right: fox
Right: rabbits
Above: grayling

☆ Canoeing   Hay-on-Wye
              Book Town ☆
              ▪ ❻
              B4351 ¦ 2 miles 🅿
              bridge   Wyeford
☆ R i v e r   W y e   car park

❺ ▪ Follow this easy-going pathway. In ⅓ mile the path begins to run parallel to your outward route and then actually merges into it.
   ▪ Keep **ahead** to a junction where the path passes beneath a road (B4351).

❻ ▪ Keep **ahead** and then drop **left** to take the narrower path, which leads back to the car park.

Walk 8 Hay-on-Wye

WALK 9

SUGAR LOAF

Sugar Loaf, or Mynydd Pen y Fâl, in Welsh, is the only real mountain walk in this book. While it's a more strenuous walk than the others, the climb to the lofty summit is hugely rewarding and well worth the effort, with stupendous views across the Black Mountains and Central Brecon Beacons, as well as over Abergavenny and the Usk Valley. To enjoy it to the full, save it for a good day and take your time on both the ascent and the descent.

OS information
SO 268167 Explorer OL13
Distance 3.8 miles/6.1km
Time 2½ hours
Start/Finish Mynydd Pen y Fâl car park
Parking NP7 7LA At the start, 2½ miles north-west of Abergavenny
Public toilets None
Cafés/pubs None (nearest in Abergavenny)
Terrain Rough hill paths that can be muddy and slippery when wet
Hilliness A 2¼-mile climb to the summit followed by a 1½-mile descent, both steep in places
Footwear Winter 🥾 Spring/Summer/Autumn (except after prolonged rain)
Public transport None
Accessibility None
Dogs Welcome, but keep on leads (livestock). No stiles

68 Short Walks Made Easy

STORIES BEHIND THE WALK

National Trust Sugar Loaf is owned by the National Trust. The organisation was founded in 1895, with an objective to safeguard places of beauty and value for the benefit of all. It has over five million members, making it Europe's largest conservation body, and it acts as guardian for over 500 historic houses and gardens, 250,000 hectares of countryside, including the national park's highest peaks of Pen y Fan and Corn Du, and around 780 miles of coastline.

Triangulation pillar When you reach the summit of Sugar Loaf, you'll be greeted by a 4-foot tall whitewashed concrete column, termed a triangulation pillar but commonly known as a trig point. These can be found on the summits of many of the Britain's hills and mountains, and on lower ground too. They were originally used by the Ordnance Survey to assist them in making accurate maps of the countryside.

Wall corner
Wall corner ½ mile
Mynydd Llanwenarth

Mynydd Pen y Fâl car park

- Walk to the interpretation signs and, with these to your right, follow the broad track that climbs away from the car park to a wall corner in ⅓ mile.
- Keep **forward** to the next wall corner.

1
- Here fork **right**. Follow this grassy path over a small crossways in about 250 yards, to reach a larger crossroads of tracks.
- Go **straight ahead**, gradually curving right with the track to a third crossways in ⅓ mile.

70 Short Walks Made Easy

✳ Sugar Loaf

At 1,955 feet above sea level, Sugar Loaf is the highest of the three outlying peaks that tower over the small town of Abergavenny, in the east of the national park. The others are: the Blorenge, which can be seen across the Usk Valley, and Ysgyryd Fawr, a few miles further east again. Sugar Loaf is a popular mountain to climb, with the high-level car park providing a great head start in getting to the top.

✳ The Black Mountains

Although not technically in the Black Mountains, Sugar Loaf is a great place from which to study the huge massif, which lies to the north. These mountains make up the easternmost range of the national park and jut to its northernmost point. The highpoint of the range, Waun Fach (2,660 feet), can be seen from this walk, although it's not easily identified, being more of a plateau than an actual peak.

2 ▶ Turn **right**. This lovely track now contours round the hillside, in ½ mile dipping into a small stream and climbing out again, and leading on to a path junction soon after, immediately ahead of a wall.

3 ▶ Turn **left**, aiming towards the summit and keep **left** at a fork in 300 yards.
▶ Climb steeply on the clear path all the way to the top to reach the whitewashed trig point.

NATURE NOTES

The common land at the foot of Sugar Loaf is a great place to see typical moorland birds such as skylarks and meadow pipits, which nest in the ling heather that covers the slopes. Skylarks are famed for their melodious song, cascading down after ascending vertically above their territories. This behaviour distinguishes them from similar-looking meadow pipits and, closer to, you can see skylark's have white tail edge feathers and small crest.

In late summer, the heather is a true spectacle in its own right, turning the steep hillsides a glorious riot of bright pinkish purple. The heather conceals red grouse, which are usually only spotted as they fly noisily away, sounding very disgruntled.

Gorse, with its bright yellow flowers, and other scrub on the lower slopes of Sugar Loaf, provide habitat for the stonechat, a robin-sized bird with dark plumage on its head and back and an attractive peachy-coloured breast. Its distinctive 'chak-chak' call can be imitated by knocking two stones together, and territorial males have been known to respond to this.

Bracken is widespread around the mountain.

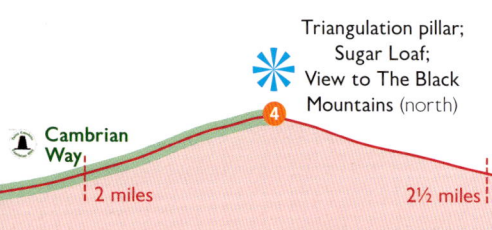

Triangulation pillar; Sugar Loaf; View to The Black Mountains (north)

Cambrian Way

2 miles

2½ miles

4 ▬ With the trig point to your back, facing in the direction of the car park, locate the main but rough, rocky track that leads diagonally downhill to the **right**.

▬ On the descent, pass a couple of side paths off right, keep **straight ahead** at a crossroads and, ignoring other side turns, meet the crossways encountered on the outward climb.

72 Short Walks Made Easy

Top: skylark
Middle: stonechat
Bottom: bracken

Top: red grouse
Bottom: heather

Wall corner — Wall corner

3 miles — 3½ miles

Mynydd Llanwenarth

Mynydd Pen y Fâl car park

5 ▪ Bear **right** and now retrace your earlier route back for ¾ mile, past the two wall corners, to the car park.

Sugar Loaf

Walk 9 Sugar Loaf 73

WALK 10

CASTLE MEADOWS

Abergavenny is one of the larger towns in the national park and is often referred to as the gateway to the Brecon Beacons. It's a bustling market town with a good selection of pubs, restaurants and independent shops, and makes a great base for exploring the area. From the railway station, this walk traces an easy-going and enthralling route across colourful water meadows, and leads on beside the beautiful River Usk before visiting the town's castle ruins.

OS information

SO 305136
Explorer OL13

Distance
2.75 miles/4.4km

Time
1½ hours

Start/Finish
Abergavenny Railway Station

Parking NP7 5HF
Bus Station car park

Public toilets
Railway Station; Bus Station car park

Cafés/pubs
Abergavenny

Terrain
Pavement; mostly well-surfaced paths; short compacted earth path

Hilliness
Mostly level; short rise/descent to/from the castle

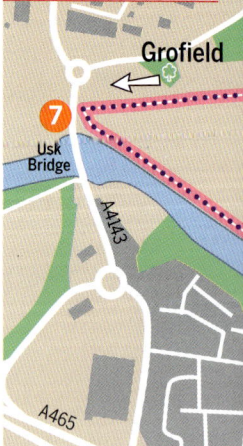

Footwear
Year round

Public transport
Mainline rail and bus and coach services to Abergavenny: traveline.cymru

Accessibility
Route is accessible except, crucially, the flight of steps at ③. Use path ③ to ⑨ or, for Castle Meadows circuit only, park at ♿ NP7 5DL

Dogs
Welcome, but keep on leads through town. No stiles

Did you know? Adolf Hitler's deputy, Rudolf Hess, was imprisoned in Abergavenny during World War II, after his failed flight to Scotland to negotiate peace in May 1941. In October 1945, Hess was taken from Abergavenny to stand trial in Nuremburg, where he was sentenced to life imprisonment. He died in Spandau Prison in 1987 having been the sole detainee there for 21 years.

Local legend The hills to the south of Abergavenny make up what has become known as Cordell Country in a tribute to Alexander Cordell, author of the Industrial Revolution-based novel, *Rape of the Fair Country*, published in 1959. The first of a trilogy, the novel depicts life in the Blaenavon Ironworks, which were located a few miles west of the town. The book was succeeded by *Hosts of Rebecca* and *Song of the Earth*.

Walk 10 Castle Meadows

STORIES BEHIND THE WALK

Abergavenny Castle Originally built by the Normans in about 1087, the castle was strategically positioned to protect the lowlands to the south and east from invasion over the mountains

by the Welsh. It's an imposing building with the present remains providing a good representation of the grandeur of the original edifice. A set of information boards explain the various sections of the building and there's also a fascinating museum within the grounds.

The Christmas Day Massacre Abergavenny Castle was once the scene of *Game of Thrones*-style massacre when, in 1175, William de Braose, a Norman lord, invited Welsh chieftain, Sitsyll ap Dyfnwal, to a Christmas Day banquet. Once seated, upon a signal the unarmed visitors were set upon and massacred by their hosts.

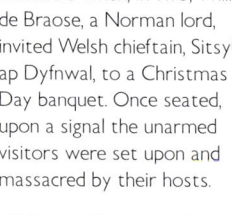

Mill Street (if starting from Bus Station, join route here; wheelchairs use path **3** to **9** — see map)

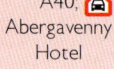

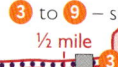

- Turn **right** out of the **Train Station** along Station Road towards light industrial units.
- Pass a bollard into an alley and follow it through to a residential road, Belmont Crescent.

1 - Continue to a T-junction and bear **right** into Holywell Crescent.
- Keep **straight on** at a crossroads into Holywell Road and walk downhill to a T-junction.

2 - Go **left** and wind down to the A40.
- Cross diagonally **left** to pass the Abergavenny Hotel then take the first **right** into Mill Street and walk to its end.
- Cross diagonally **right** to a flight of stone steps behind a wall.

☆ Abergavenny

amed after the confluence of e Nant Fenni with the River sk (both visited during this alk), Abergavenny is a lively wn with good rail and bus ks. The town sprung up ound a Roman fort and later came a walled town within e Welsh Marches. Today it s an excellent reputation nong foodies and hosts an nual food fair.

☆ Castle Meadows

Close to the centre of town, Castle Meadows comprise 50 acres of grassland alongside the River Usk. They are dotted with small ponds and irrigated by many small streams, including the Nant Fenni, from which the town takes its name. The meadows are criss-crossed with an excellent network of paths, including a beautiful stretch along the river bank, and are overseen by the castle on one side and the imposing bulk of the mountain, Blorenge, on the other.

Abergavenny Castle

Castle rampart

Usk Bridge (ahead)

1 mile Byefield Lane car park

☆ Castle Meadows

Bus Station
➥ From the Bus Station car park, walk out to the A40 entrance/exit, turn **right** then go first **left** down Mill Street to the flight of stone steps in 100 yards.

3 ➥ Climb the steps and follow the path round beneath the castle walls before swinging **right** to climb the lane to the castle gates.

4 ➥ After taking in the ruins, return through the gates and turn **left** down Castle Street to a fork in 75 yards.

NATURE NOTES

In spring and summer, Castle Meadows are particularly colourful, with large swathes of buttercups lining the River Usk, and marsh marigolds and yellow flag irises punctuating the many small ponds.

The ponds are great places to spot insects too, such as water boatmen, whirligig beetles and pond skaters. Watch patiently and an insect menagerie can appear.

The meadows are also dotted with many trees including beech, oak, willow, rowan and horse chestnut, whose attractive candelabra-like flowers in spring are followed by prickly-cased conkers in the autumn.

Mallard ducks abound on the Usk, where you might also see fly fishermen casting for salmon and trout. Kingfishers also fish the stiller pools on the river, while sand martins, migrants from Africa that can arrive as early as March, nest in burrows in the sandy riverbanks. Back on the meadows, very pretty goldfinches may be found searching for dandelion, thistle and teasel seeds.

☆ River Usk

1½ miles

Footbridge

8

2 miles

5 ➡ Keep **right** and pass a concrete bollard, walking downhill and turning **right** onto a well-surfaced footpath at the bottom.

➡ Follow this through trees and out onto open ground, keeping ahead with a tree-lined stream (left) to pass Byefield Lane car park (right).

Byefield Lane car park
Exit from the bottom of the car park onto the grass and turn **right** for a circuit of Castle Meadows.

6 ➡ Continue **straight ahead** to the end of the fence on your right.

➡ Turn **right** and then **left** onto another clear path that leads across the meadows to the far corner by an impressive stone road bridge.

Short Walks Made Easy